WELCOME TO THE U.S.A.
NEW JERSEY

Written by Ann Heinrichs   Illustrated by Matt Kania
Content Adviser: Howard L. Green, Research Director, New Jersey
Historical Commission, Highland Park, New Jersey

The Child's World

Published in the United States of America by The Child's World®
PO Box 326 • Chanhassen, MN 55317-0326
800-599-READ • www.childsworld.com

Photo Credits

Cover: Photodisc; frontispiece: Getty Images/Stone/Don Spiro.

Interior: Marvin and Lori Blethen/Bridgeton Reenaissance League: 13; Corbis:
17 (Ted Spiegel), 18 (Lee Snider/Photo Images), 29 (Dave G. Houser), 30
(Bob Krist), 35 (Joseph Sohm/ChromoSohm Inc.); Kelly-Mooney Photography/
Corbis: 6, 10, 14, 22; Liberty Science Center: 26; Library of Congress: 16,
35; Ridgewood Historical Society/The Schoolhouse Museum: 25; Save Lucy
Committee: 9; Wheaton Village: 21; Whitesbog Preservation Society: 33.

Acknowledgments

The Child's World®: Mary Berendes, Publishing Director

Editorial Directions, Inc.: E. Russell Primm, Editorial Director; Katie Marsico, Associate
Editor; Judith Shiffer, Assistant Editor; Matt Messbarger, Editorial Assistant; Susan
Hindman, Copy Editor; Melissa McDaniel, Proofreader; Kevin Cunningham, Peter
Garnham, Matt Messbarger, Olivia Nellums, Chris Simms, Molly Symmonds, Katherine
Trickle, Carl Stephen Wender, Fact Checkers; Tim Griffin/IndexServ, Indexer; Cian
Loughlin O'Day, Photo Researcher and Editor

The Design Lab: Kathleen Petelinsek, Design and art production

Library of Congress Cataloging-in-Publication Data
Heinrichs, Ann.
New Jersey / by Ann Heinrichs.
p. cm. — (Welcome to the U.S.A.)
Includes index.
ISBN 1-59296-378-1 (library bound : alk. paper) 1. New Jersey—Juvenile literature.
I. Title. II. Series.
F134.3.H45 2006
974.9'01—dc22   2004026170

Ann Heinrichs is the author of more than 100 books for children and young adults. She has also enjoyed successful careers as a children's book editor and an advertising copywriter. Ann grew up in Fort Smith, Arkansas, and lives in Chicago, Illinois.

About the Author
Ann Heinrichs

Matt Kania loves maps and, as a kid, dreamed of making them. In school he studied geography and cartography, and today he makes maps for a living. Matt's favorite thing about drawing maps is learning about the places they represent. Many of the maps he has created can be found in books, magazines, videos, Web sites, and public places.

About the
Map Illustrator
Matt Kania

On the cover: People come to Atlantic City for the beach, boardwalk, and casinos.
On page one: Farms such as this one in Lafayette raise blueberries and other foods.

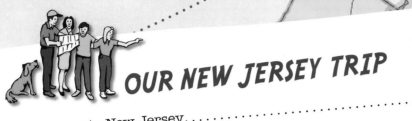

OUR NEW JERSEY TRIP

New Jersey's Nickname: The Garden State

WELCOME TO NEW JERSEY

All aboard for the Garden State. That's New Jersey! There's so much to see and do there. And lots to learn, too. Here's a taste of what's to come.

You'll meet Thomas Edison and Lucy the Elephant. You'll watch George Washington cross the Delaware River. You'll gobble up blueberry pies. You'll make glass with a master glassmaker. And you'll climb a lighthouse named Old Barney.

That's a lot of stuff for one trip. So we'd better hit the road. Just buckle up, and we're on our way!

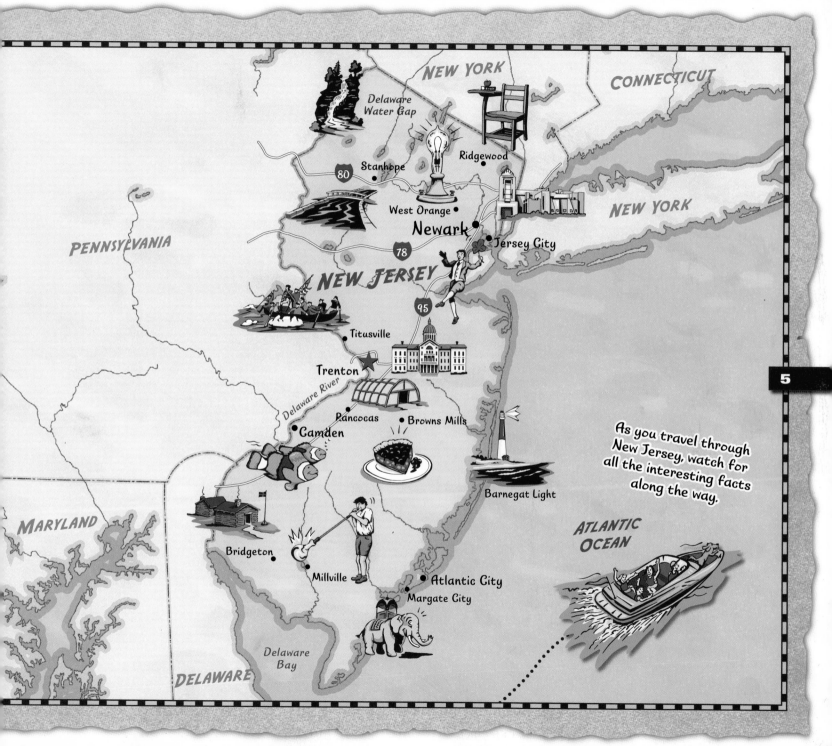

NEW YORK

CONNECTICUT

Delaware
Water Gap

Ridgewood

Stanhope
80

NEW YORK

West Orange

Newark

Jersey City

PENNSYLVANIA

78

NEW JERSEY

95

Titusville

Trenton

Delaware River

Rancocas

Browns Mills

Camden

Barnegat Light

As you travel through
New Jersey, watch for
all the interesting facts
along the way.

MARYLAND

Bridgeton

ATLANTIC
OCEAN

Millville

Atlantic City

Margate City

Delaware
Bay

DELAWARE

5

Take a boat ride on the Delaware River! You're sure to enjoy New Jersey's scenic wilderness.

Millbrook Village lies along the Delaware Water Gap. It's an 1800s village. It has a school, church, farmhouses, and many old shops.

Drift down the river in a boat. High mountains tower above you on both sides. Or hike through the lush forest. You'll come across lakes, ponds, and waterfalls.

This deep valley is the Delaware Water Gap. It's a place to enjoy nature and outdoor fun. The Delaware River flows through this **gorge.** The river carved out the gorge over millions of years.

The Delaware River forms New Jersey's western border. Most of eastern New Jersey faces the Atlantic Ocean. Lots of sandy beaches line the shore. Northeastern New Jersey faces the Hudson River. This area has many busy port cities. New York City lies just across the Hudson.

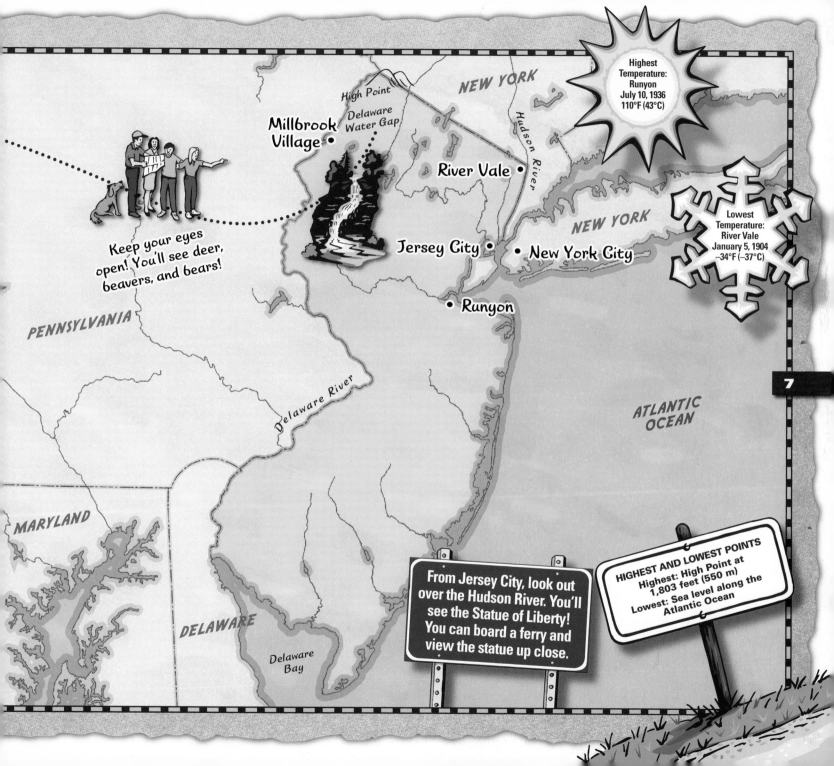

NEW YORK

High Point

Delaware
Water Gap

Millbrook
Village

River Vale

Hudson River

NEW YORK

Jersey City

New York City

Runyon

Keep your eyes
open! You'll see deer,
beavers, and bears!

PENNSYLVANIA

Highest Temperature:
Runyon
July 10, 1936
110°F (43°C)

Lowest Temperature:
River Vale
January 5, 1904
−34°F (−37°C)

Delaware River

ATLANTIC
OCEAN

MARYLAND

DELAWARE

Delaware
Bay

From Jersey City, look out
over the Hudson River. You'll
see the Statue of Liberty!
You can board a ferry and
view the statue up close.

HIGHEST AND LOWEST POINTS
Highest: High Point at
1,803 feet (550 m)
Lowest: Sea level along the
Atlantic Ocean

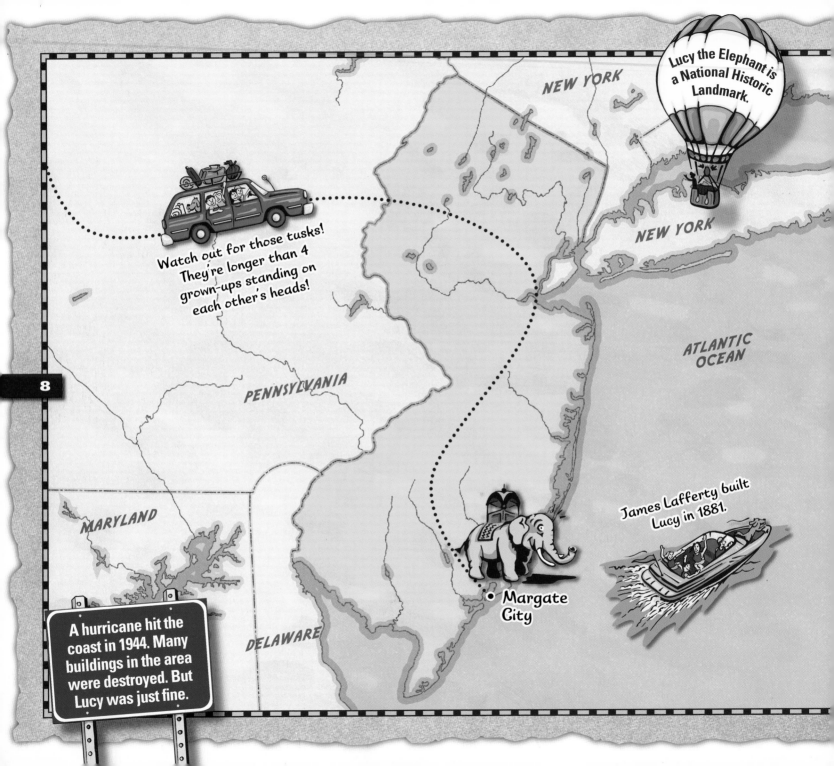

NEW YORK

Lucy the Elephant is a National Historic Landmark.

NEW YORK

Watch out for those tusks! They're longer than 4 grown-ups standing on each other's heads!

ATLANTIC OCEAN

PENNSYLVANIA

James Lafferty built Lucy in 1881.

MARYLAND

● Margate City

A hurricane hit the coast in 1944. Many buildings in the area were destroyed. But Lucy was just fine.

DELAWARE

Climbing Lucy the Elephant in Margate City

Want to see the world through an elephant's eyes? Just climb up inside Lucy the Elephant. Then look out the windows in her head. They are her eyes!

Lucy the Elephant stands on Margate beach. She's taller than a six-story building. She weighs as much as ten real elephants.

Are you at the circus? No, you're just visiting Lucy in Margate City!

Once you're inside Lucy, you'll walk up a winding staircase. You'll see that Lucy's all pink inside. The main room has a TV. You can watch videos about Lucy.

Sometimes **hurricanes** smash against Lucy. But she just keeps standing. She's been there for more than 120 years!

In 1902, a family lived in Lucy. She was their summer home.

A Native American dancer performs at Rancocas.

10

Check out the American Indian Heritage Museum. It's on what its organizers call the Rankokus Indian **Reservation.** Your guides are real Indians. They tell you about the history and **culture** of many different Indian groups.

Inside, large displays show scenes from every-day life. Outside, there's an American Indian village. The longhouse there is a typical woodland Indian home.

Thousands of American Indians once lived in New Jersey. They were the Lenape, or Lenni-Lenape. Europeans called them the Delaware.

European explorers began arriving in the 1500s. Giovanni da Verrazano sailed to the coast in 1524. Henry Hudson arrived in 1609.

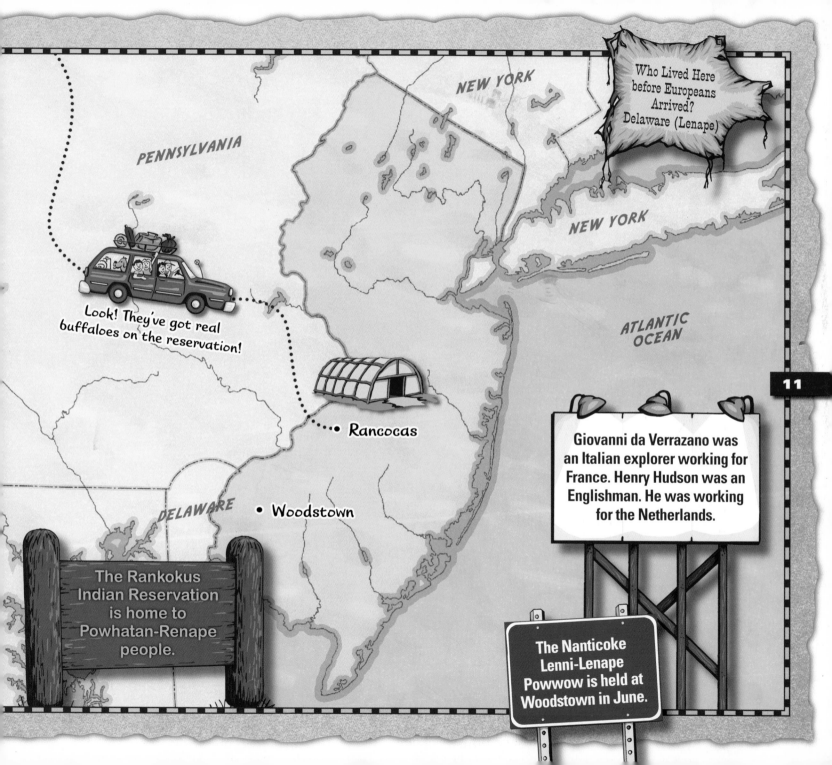

Who Lived Here before Europeans Arrived? Delaware (Lenape)

PENNSYLVANIA

NEW YORK

ATLANTIC OCEAN

Look! They've got real buffaloes on the reservation!

Rancocas

DELAWARE

Woodstown

Giovanni da Verrazano was an Italian explorer working for France. Henry Hudson was an Englishman. He was working for the Netherlands.

The Rankokus Indian Reservation is home to Powhatan-Renape people.

The Nanticoke Lenni-Lenape Powwow is held at Woodstown in June.

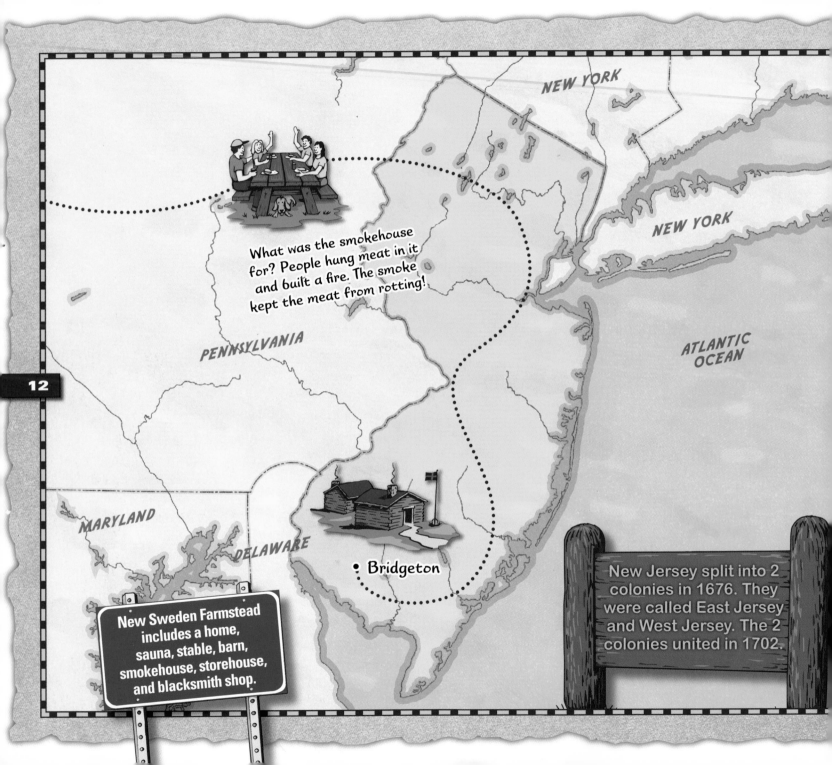

NEW YORK

NEW YORK

What was the smokehouse for? People hung meat in it and built a fire. The smoke kept the meat from rotting!

PENNSYLVANIA

ATLANTIC OCEAN

MARYLAND

DELAWARE

• Bridgeton

New Sweden Farmstead includes a home, sauna, stable, barn, smokehouse, storehouse, and blacksmith shop.

New Jersey split into 2 colonies in 1676. They were called East Jersey and West Jersey. The 2 colonies united in 1702.

Performers reenact a 17th-century Christmas at New Sweden Farmstead.

Have you ever had a sauna? That's a kind of steam bath. Water is poured over heated rocks. Then the water turns into steam!

You'll see a sauna at New Sweden Farmstead. You'll also see barns and many other buildings. They show life in an early **colony.**

Dutch people settled in New Jersey in 1630. Settlers from Sweden and Finland came in 1638. They formed a colony called New Sweden. England took over the region in 1664.

New Jersey's English governors allowed religious freedom. Many English religious groups sailed to New Jersey. There they were free to practice their faith.

Gee . . . those bagpipes are hard to play. You blow air into the bag and push it out with your arm. Meanwhile, you play a tune.

14

Bagpipes are blaring. Grown men are wearing plaid skirts. And everybody's in green. It's the Saint Patrick's Day Parade in Newark! That's a big Irish holiday.

New Jersey's people belong to many **ethnic** groups. It would be hard to name them all! Many came from Italy. Some came from Ireland, Germany, or Russia. Others came from Scotland, Sweden, Poland, or Greece. More recently, many people in New Jersey claim Mexican, Puerto Rican, African, or Asian roots. Each group has its special music, crafts, and foods.

This woman is in traditional African dress. She's attending an ethnic festival in Holmdel.

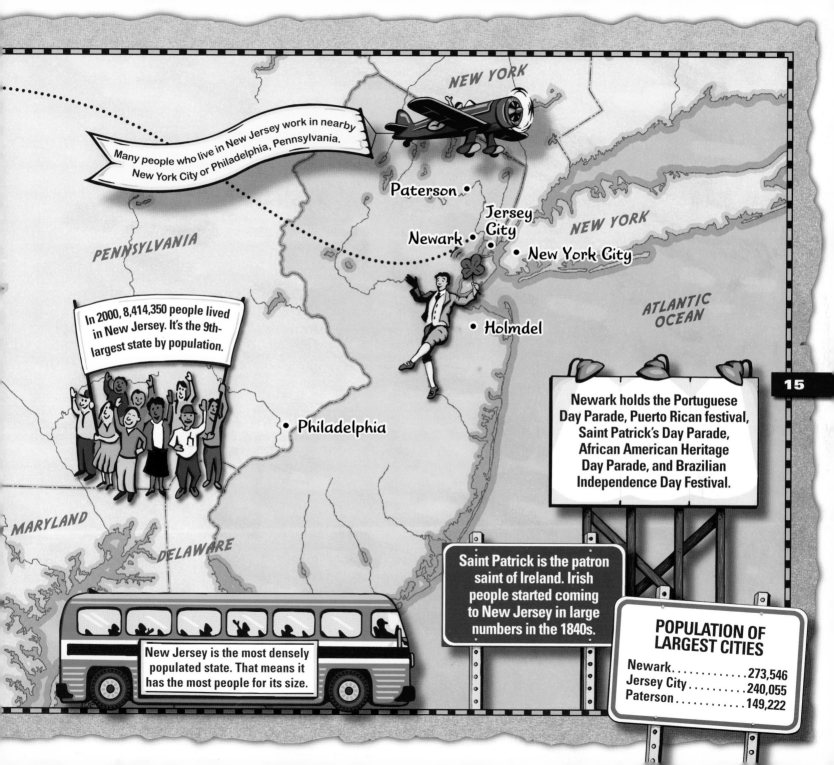

Many people who live in New Jersey work in nearby New York City or Philadelphia, Pennsylvania.

In 2000, 8,414,350 people lived in New Jersey. It's the 9th-largest state by population.

NEW YORK

PENNSYLVANIA

Paterson

Jersey City

Newark

New York City

NEW YORK

ATLANTIC OCEAN

Holmdel

Philadelphia

MARYLAND

DELAWARE

15

Newark holds the Portuguese Day Parade, Puerto Rican festival, Saint Patrick's Day Parade, African American Heritage Day Parade, and Brazilian Independence Day Festival.

Saint Patrick is the patron saint of Ireland. Irish people started coming to New Jersey in large numbers in the 1840s.

New Jersey is the most densely populated state. That means it has the most people for its size.

POPULATION OF LARGEST CITIES

Newark. 273,546
Jersey City 240,055
Paterson 149,222

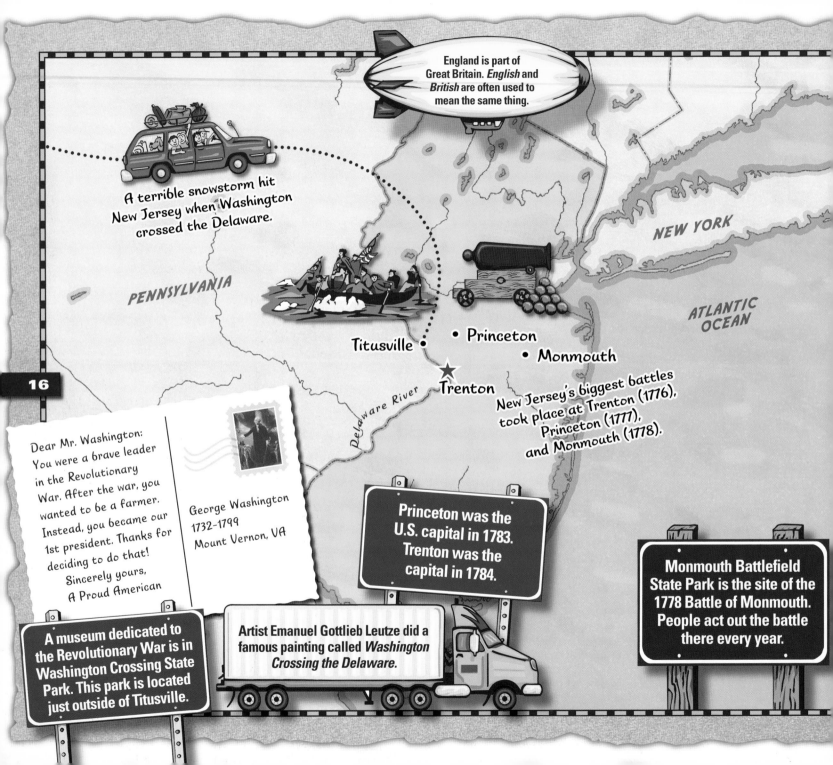

England is part of Great Britain. *English* and *British* are often used to mean the same thing.

A terrible snowstorm hit New Jersey when Washington crossed the Delaware.

NEW YORK

PENNSYLVANIA

ATLANTIC OCEAN

Titusville

Princeton

Monmouth

Delaware River

★ Trenton

New Jersey's biggest battles took place at Trenton (1776), Princeton (1777), and Monmouth (1778).

Dear Mr. Washington:
You were a brave leader in the Revolutionary War. After the war, you wanted to be a farmer. Instead, you became our 1st president. Thanks for deciding to do that!
Sincerely yours,
A Proud American

George Washington
1732–1799
Mount Vernon, VA

Princeton was the U.S. capital in 1783. Trenton was the capital in 1784.

Monmouth Battlefield State Park is the site of the 1778 Battle of Monmouth. People act out the battle there every year.

A museum dedicated to the Revolutionary War is in Washington Crossing State Park. This park is located just outside of Titusville.

Artist Emanuel Gottlieb Leutze did a famous painting called *Washington Crossing the Delaware.*

Washington's Crossing at Titusville

It's Christmastime in Titusville. It's cold and snowy. You stand by the Delaware River, waiting. At last, you see the boat coming. It's George Washington! Well, it's not really George. It's a man dressed like him. He's acting out a famous event in history.

The colonies wanted freedom from Great Britain. So they fought the Revolutionary War (1775–1783). George Washington led the colonies' soldiers. On Christmas, enemy troops camped at Trenton. Washington's camp was across the Delaware River. No one would expect an attack on Christmas. So Washington crossed the Delaware late at night. His surprise attack was a big success! And so was the war.

Watch out—that water looks chilly! Performers reenact Washington crossing the Delaware River.

New Jersey was the 3rd state to enter the Union. It joined on December 18, 1787.

The state capitol has a shiny golden dome. You can see it from far away. It glistens in the sun. It seems to be saying, "This building is important!"

Well, it *is* important. The capitol is the center of the state government.

New Jersey's government is divided into three branches. One branch makes the state's laws. It consists of a senate and a general assembly. Another branch makes sure people obey the laws. The governor is the head of this branch. And a third branch is made up of judges. They decide whether laws have been broken.

Look up! You're standing inside the capitol in Trenton.

Welcome to
Trenton, the
capital of
New Jersey!

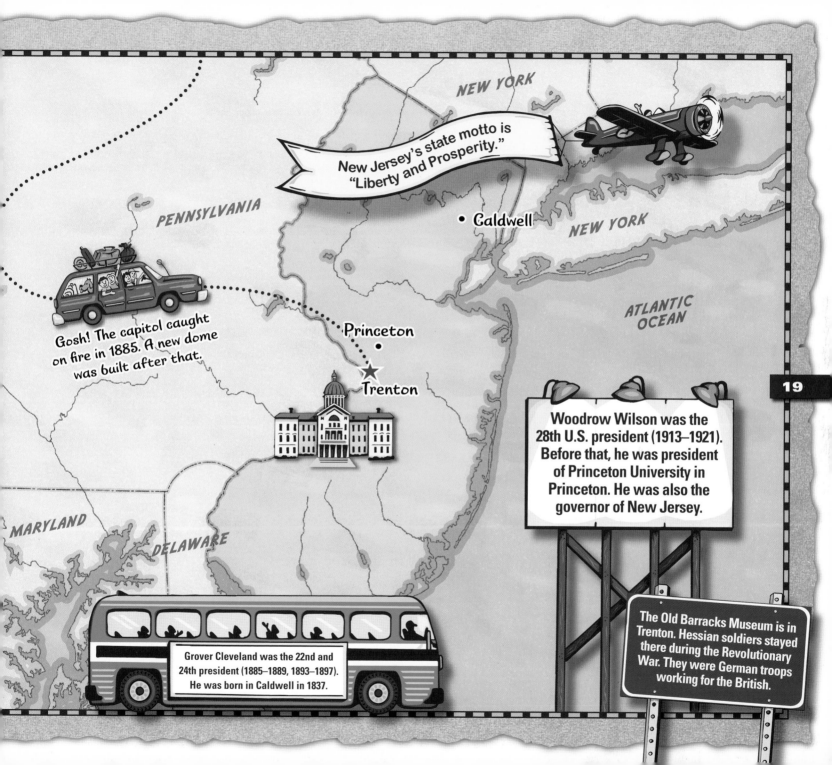

NEW YORK

New Jersey's state motto is "Liberty and Prosperity."

PENNSYLVANIA

• Caldwell

NEW YORK

ATLANTIC OCEAN

Gosh! The capitol caught on fire in 1885. A new dome was built after that.

Princeton
•

★ Trenton

Woodrow Wilson was the 28th U.S. president (1913–1921). Before that, he was president of Princeton University in Princeton. He was also the governor of New Jersey.

MARYLAND

DELAWARE

Grover Cleveland was the 22nd and 24th president (1885–1889, 1893–1897). He was born in Caldwell in 1837.

The Old Barracks Museum is in Trenton. Hessian soldiers stayed there during the Revolutionary War. They were German troops working for the British.

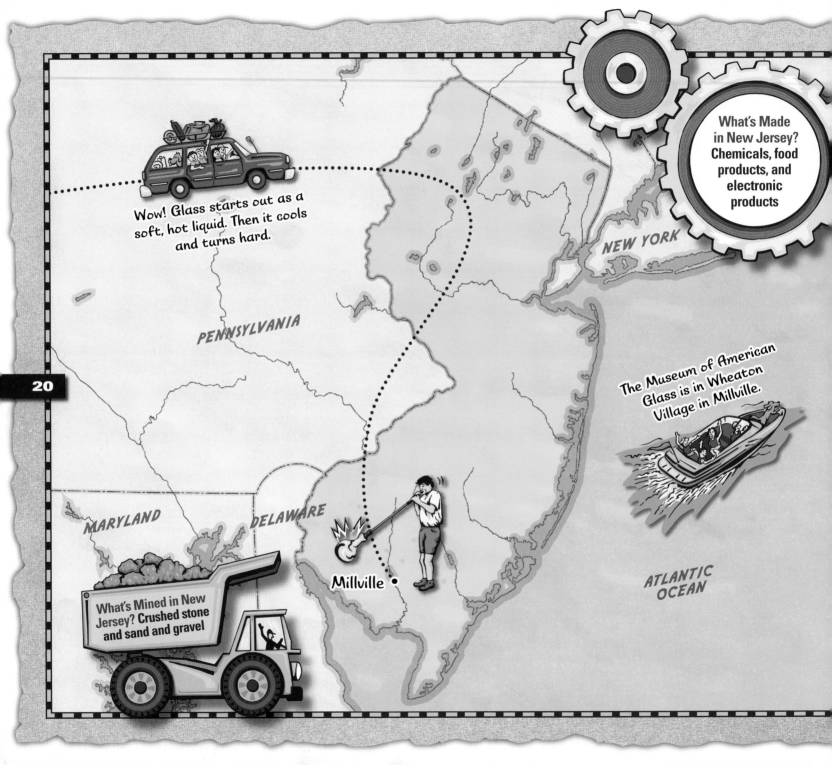

Wow! Glass starts out as a soft, hot liquid. Then it cools and turns hard.

What's Made in New Jersey? Chemicals, food products, and electronic products

NEW YORK

PENNSYLVANIA

The Museum of American Glass is in Wheaton Village in Millville.

MARYLAND

DELAWARE

Millville •

What's Mined in New Jersey? Crushed stone and sand and gravel

ATLANTIC OCEAN

How would you like to make a glass **paperweight**? Just take a tour of Wheaton Glass Factory.

You'll see master artists blowing big glass bubbles. You'll watch them bend and shape the glass. It seems like magic! Finally, you'll get to make your own paperweight.

Even in the 1700s, New Jersey had busy factories. These factories were small and only a few people worked in each. They made cloth and many other products. Today, some big factories are still chugging away. Their products include medicines, foods, and electronic products.

Would you enjoy working at the Wheaton Glass Factory? This artist is blowing glass.

21

Southern New Jersey once had many glass-making towns.

Ever wonder how a broom is made? Just talk to the workers at Waterloo Village!

22

Ever heard of an inclined plane? It's a long, slanted surface. People use them for sliding things up and down. You'll see an inclined plane at Stanhope's Waterloo Village. Boats used to slide on it.

Western New Jersey produced lots of iron. People needed to ship the iron eastward. So they dug the Morris Canal. It joined the Delaware and Hudson rivers. People could ship tons of products on canal boats.

There was only one problem. The canal went over hilly land. Boats could not sail uphill. So they were moved upward on inclined planes.

Waterloo Village was a busy canal town. You'll see its blacksmith shop, school, stores, and homes.

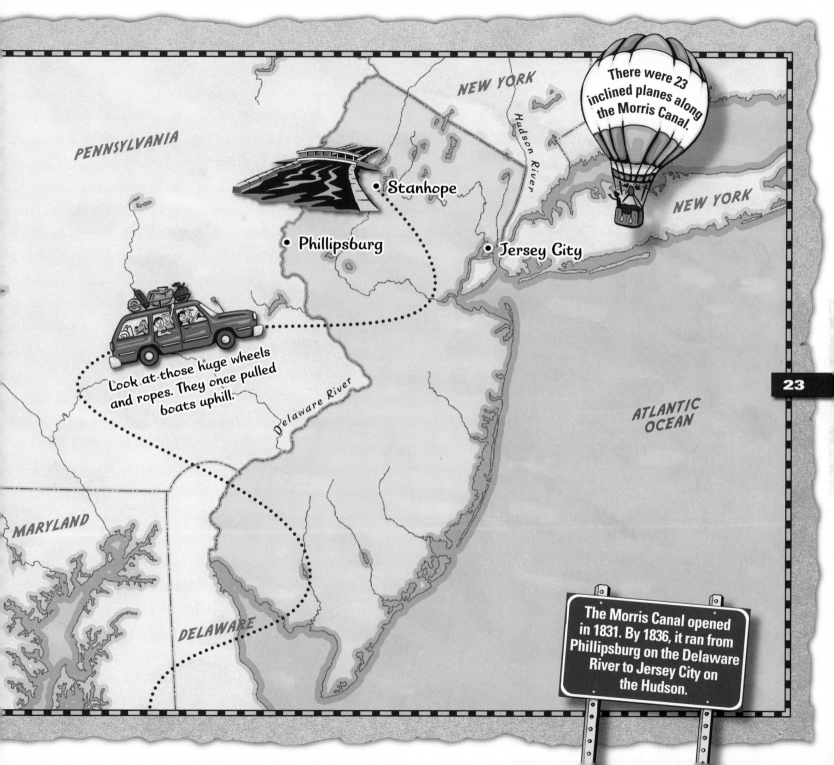

NEW YORK

PENNSYLVANIA

Hudson River

There were 23 inclined planes along the Morris Canal.

NEW YORK

• Stanhope

• Phillipsburg

• Jersey City

Look at those huge wheels and ropes. They once pulled boats uphill.

Delaware River

ATLANTIC OCEAN

MARYLAND

DELAWARE

The Morris Canal opened in 1831. By 1836, it ran from Phillipsburg on the Delaware River to Jersey City on the Hudson.

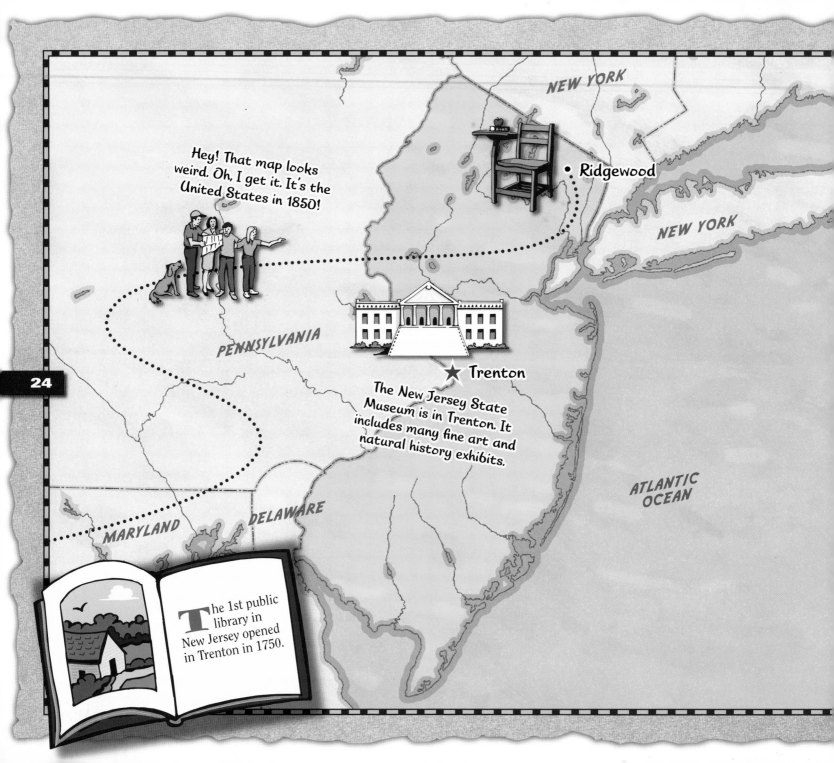

Hey! That map looks weird. Oh, I get it. It's the United States in 1850!

NEW YORK

Ridgewood

NEW YORK

ATLANTIC OCEAN

The New Jersey State Museum is in Trenton. It includes many fine art and natural history exhibits.

★ Trenton

PENNSYLVANIA

MARYLAND

DELAWARE

The 1st public library in New Jersey opened in Trenton in 1750.

The Schoolhouse Museum in Ridgewood

What was school like 150 years ago? Visit the Schoolhouse Museum, and you'll see. There's a potbellied stove for heat. There are reading charts, desks, and maps.

And what's that in the corner? It's a tall stool. That's where naughty kids had to sit. They had to wear a tall, pointy hat. Maybe your school's not so bad after all!

This one-room schoolhouse is a great museum. It displays more than school materials. There are spinning wheels and handmade toys. There's a kitchen from the 1700s. Look around and imagine living back then. Would you have liked it?

You'll receive a lesson in history at Ridgewood's Schoolhouse Museum.

Would you make a good scientist? Visit Liberty Science Center and find out!

Thomas Edison invented electric lightbulbs. Alfred Vail helped develop the telegraph. And Albert Einstein figured out a lot about the universe. All 3 worked in New Jersey!

Liberty Science Center in Jersey City

What will you look like in five years? Ten years? Fifteen years? Want to talk with a doctor during surgery? Want to see your hair stand straight out? Visit the Liberty Science Center!

Many scientists work in New Jersey. The state's scientists found many uses for chemicals especially in the 1950s. The most valuable chemicals are medicines. Others include shampoos, soaps, and paint.

Would you like to be a scientist one day? Then Liberty Science Center is a great place to visit. Even science teachers learn a lot there.

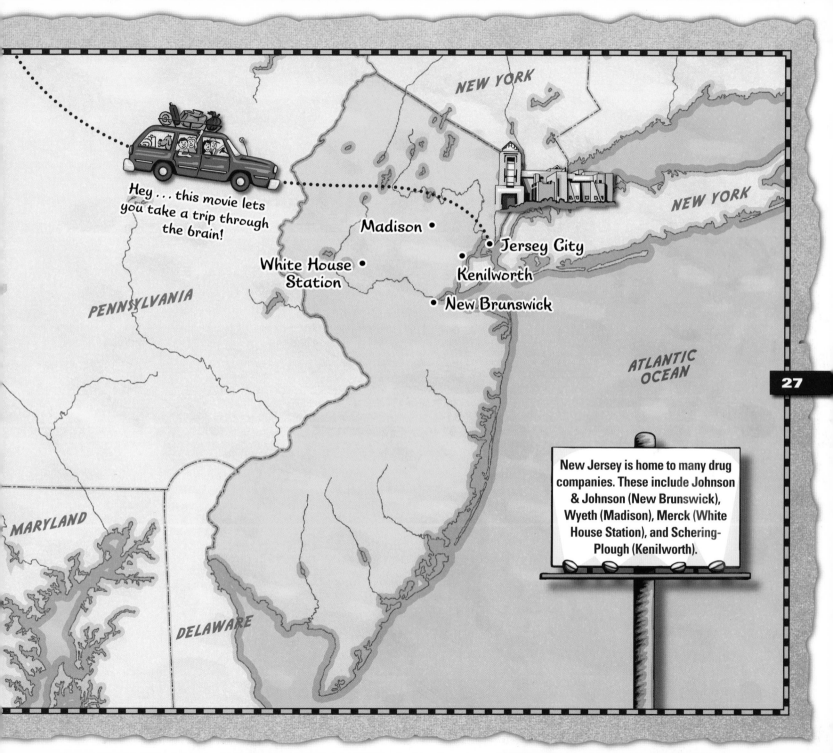

Hey . . . this movie lets you take a trip through the brain!

NEW YORK

NEW YORK

Madison •

White House Station •

• Jersey City

Kenilworth

• New Brunswick

PENNSYLVANIA

ATLANTIC OCEAN

MARYLAND

DELAWARE

New Jersey is home to many drug companies. These include Johnson & Johnson (New Brunswick), Wyeth (Madison), Merck (White House Station), and Schering-Plough (Kenilworth).

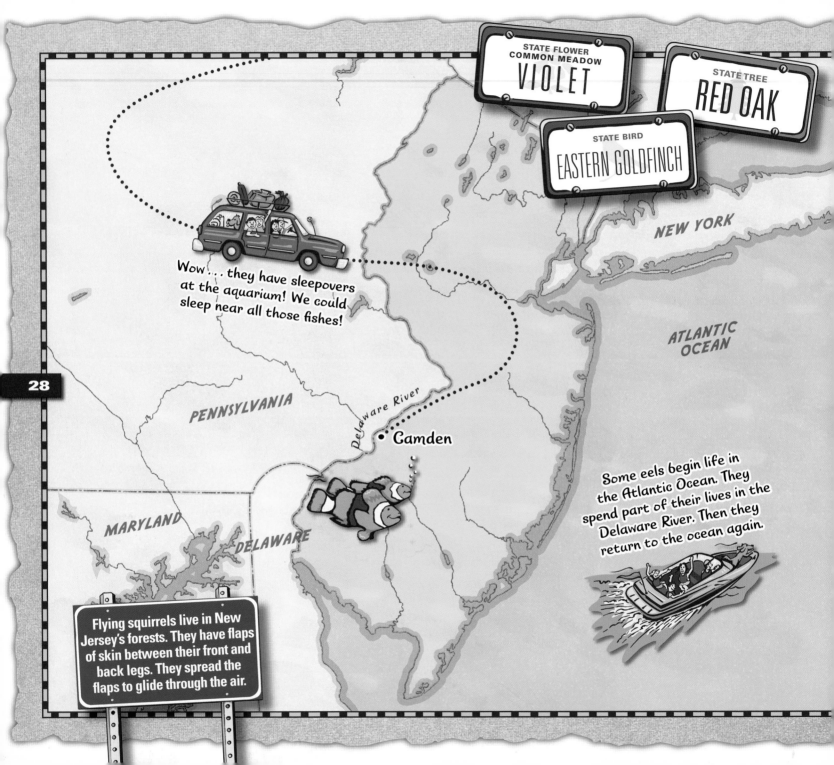

STATE FLOWER
COMMON MEADOW
VIOLET

STATE TREE
RED OAK

STATE BIRD
EASTERN GOLDFINCH

NEW YORK

ATLANTIC OCEAN

Wow.... they have sleepovers at the aquarium! We could sleep near all those fishes!

PENNSYLVANIA

Delaware River

• Camden

MARYLAND

DELAWARE

Some eels begin life in the Atlantic Ocean. They spend part of their lives in the Delaware River. Then they return to the ocean again.

Flying squirrels live in New Jersey's forests. They have flaps of skin between their front and back legs. They spread the flaps to glide through the air.

Step inside to learn all about fish! You're touring the New Jersey State Aquarium in Camden.

Want to touch a stingray? Want to watch seals doing tricks? How about a sleepover among the fish tanks? Just drop by the New Jersey State Aquarium. There's plenty of fun stuff going on there!

This aquarium explores the world's sea life. Some animals there come from New Jersey waters. Others come from far away. One example is a four-eyed fish!

Clams, crabs, and lobsters live off New Jersey's coast. Plenty of fish swim in the rivers and streams. The forests have lots of wildlife, too. There you'll see chipmunks and squirrels. You might see deer, foxes, bears, and rabbits, too. Just watch out for skunks!

The National Park Service has 9 sites in New Jersey.

29

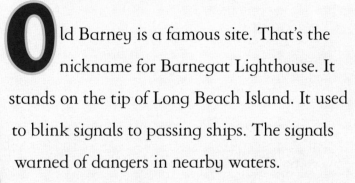

Planning on taking a boat trip? Old Barney will guide you safely to shore.

Old Barney is a famous site. That's the nickname for Barnegat Lighthouse. It stands on the tip of Long Beach Island. It used to blink signals to passing ships. The signals warned of dangers in nearby waters.

You can climb up inside Old Barney. Look around—you can see for miles. Lots of people visit lighthouses as a hobby.

Strolling along New Jersey's beaches is fun, too. There are many seaside vacation towns. Atlantic City is a famous beach town. So are Cape May, Ocean City, and Seaside Heights. Many beaches have boardwalks. They are just what they sound like—wooden sidewalks!

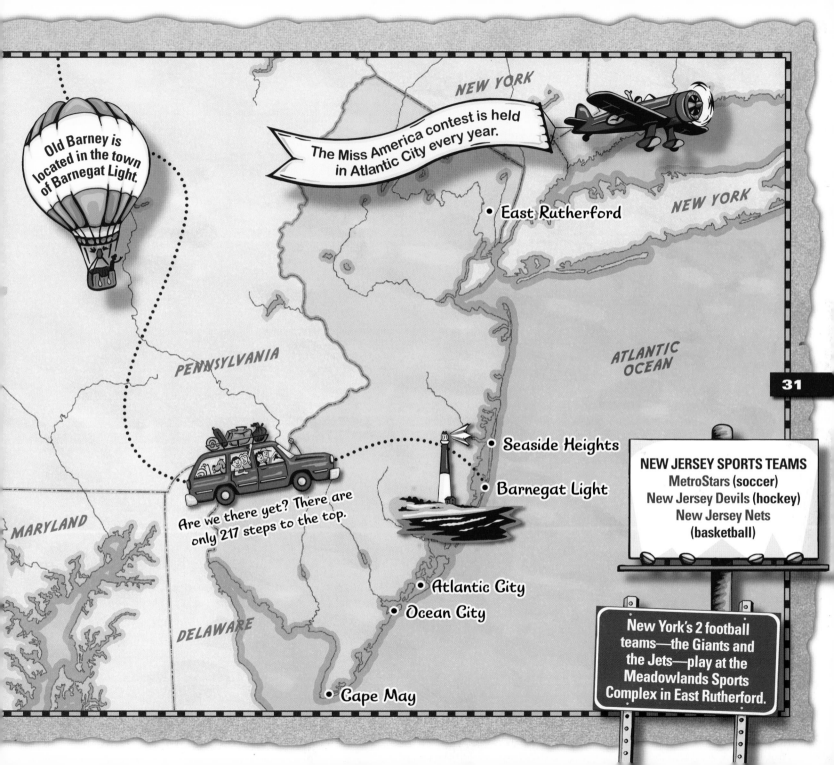

Old Barney is located in the town of Barnegat Light.

The Miss America contest is held in Atlantic City every year.

NEW YORK

East Rutherford

NEW YORK

PENNSYLVANIA

ATLANTIC OCEAN

Are we there yet? There are only 217 steps to the top.

Seaside Heights

Barnegat Light

MARYLAND

NEW JERSEY SPORTS TEAMS
MetroStars (soccer)
New Jersey Devils (hockey)
New Jersey Nets
(basketball)

Atlantic City

Ocean City

DELAWARE

New York's 2 football teams—the Giants and the Jets—play at the Meadowlands Sports Complex in East Rutherford.

Cape May

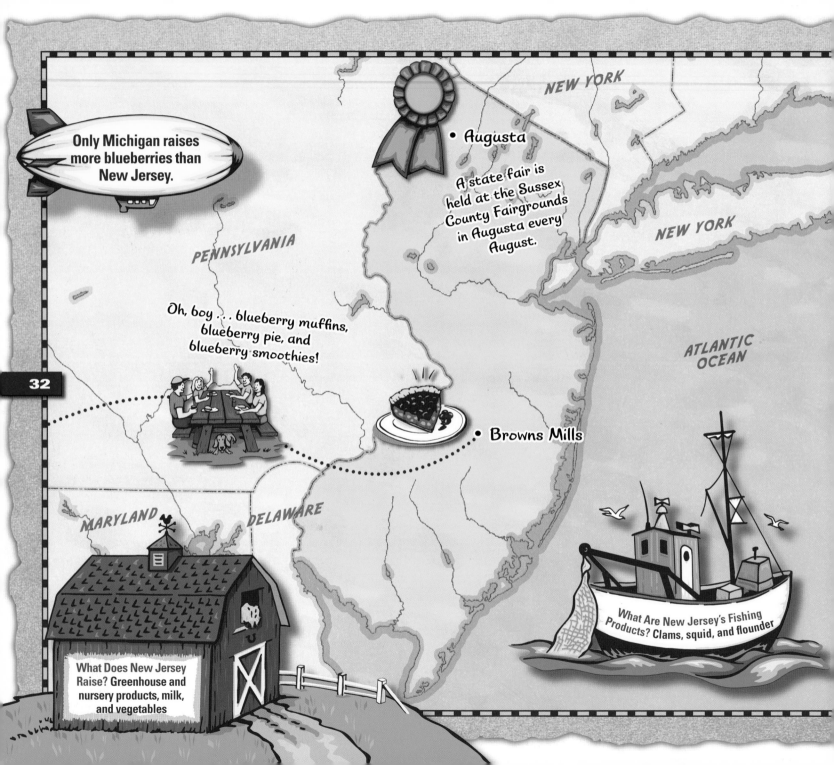

How many blueberry pies can you eat? Just stop by the Whitesbog Blueberry Festival. It celebrates New Jersey's state fruit— the blueberry. One fun event is the blueberry pie-eating contest!

New Jersey raises lots of fruits and vegetables. It's a leading state for blueberries and cranberries. But flowers are the state's top crop. In fact, New Jersey is called the Garden State. It grows millions of roses, lilies, and geraniums.

Fishing is another big **industry** in New Jersey. Tons of clams are caught off the coast. So are lobsters, crabs, squid, and fish.

Yum! This young champion won the pie-eating contest at Browns Mills.

Farmers began raising blueberries in Whitesbog in 1916. Before that, the blueberries grew wild.

Thomas Edison once lived in this house in West Orange.

34

The Edison National Historic Site is in West Orange. It preserves Edison's home and lab.

Where would you be without Thomas Edison? You'd be in the dark, that's where! Edison invented electric lightbulbs. Edison was an awesome inventor. He invented 1,093 new things! One was the phonograph record player. Another was motion pictures.

Edison's first **laboratory** was in Menlo Park. He built an even bigger lab in 1887. It was in West Orange. Edison called this new lab the Invention Factory. You'll see many of his inventions there. Maybe they'll give you some bright ideas!

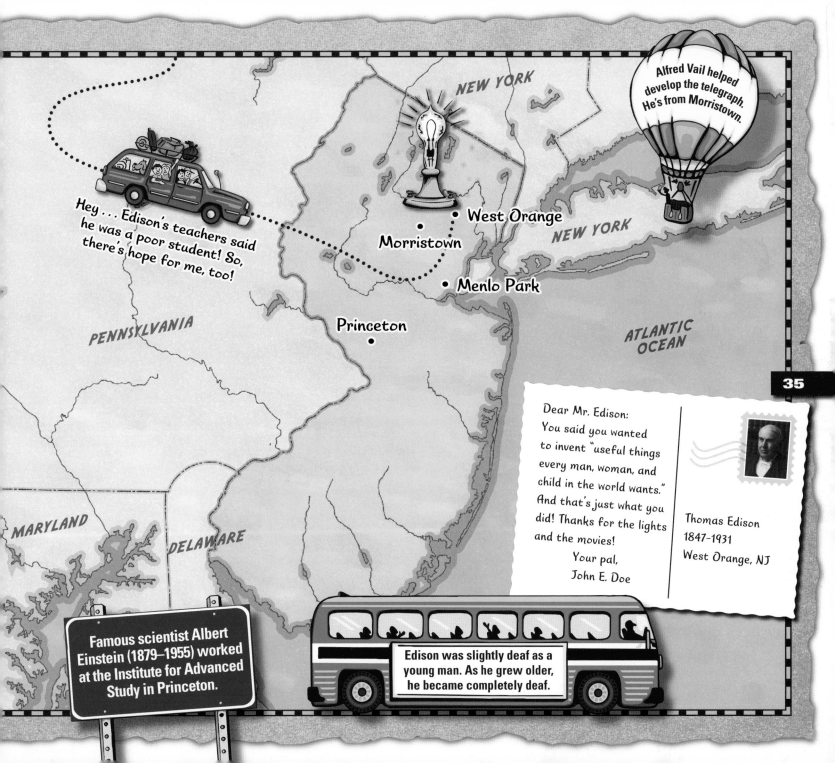

NEW YORK

Alfred Vail helped develop the telegraph. He's from Morristown.

Hey . . . Edison's teachers said he was a poor student! So, there's hope for me, too!

West Orange

Morristown

NEW YORK

Menlo Park

Princeton

PENNSYLVANIA

ATLANTIC OCEAN

Dear Mr. Edison:
You said you wanted to invent "useful things every man, woman, and child in the world wants." And that's just what you did! Thanks for the lights and the movies!

Your pal,
John E. Doe

Thomas Edison
1847–1931
West Orange, NJ

MARYLAND

DELAWARE

Famous scientist Albert Einstein (1879–1955) worked at the Institute for Advanced Study in Princeton.

Edison was slightly deaf as a young man. As he grew older, he became completely deaf.

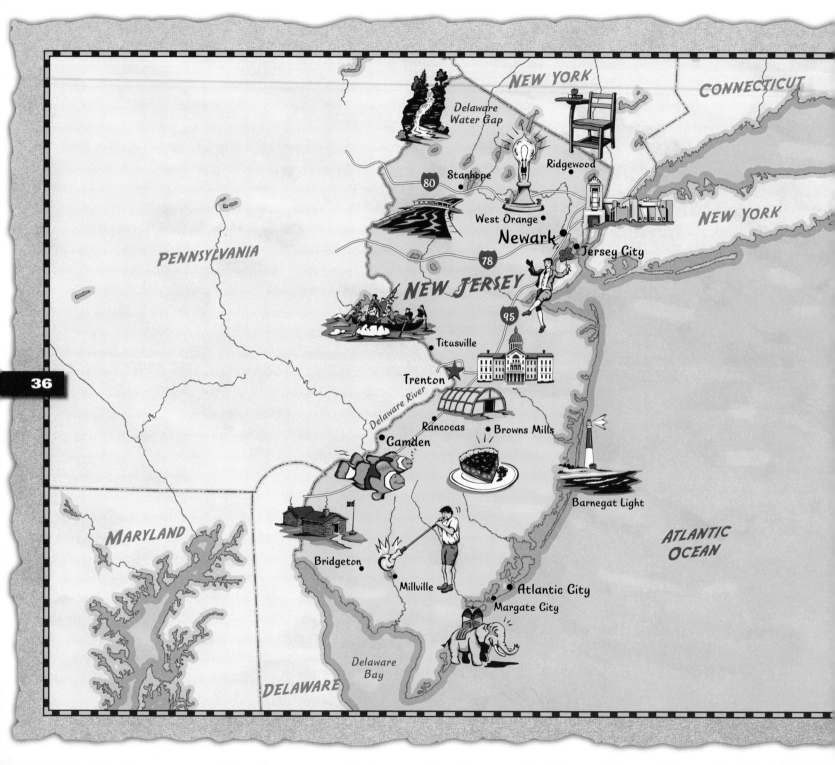

NEW YORK

CONNECTICUT

Delaware
Water Gap

Ridgewood

80 Stanhope

NEW YORK

West Orange

Newark

Jersey City

PENNSYLVANIA

78

NEW JERSEY

95

Titusville

Trenton

Delaware River

Rancocas

Camden

Browns Mills

Barnegat Light

MARYLAND

ATLANTIC
OCEAN

Bridgeton

Millville

Atlantic City

Margate City

Delaware
Bay

DELAWARE

OUR TRIP

We visited many places on our trip! We also met a lot of interesting people along the way. Look at the map on the left. Use your finger to trace all the places we have been.

Who built Lucy the Elephant? See page 8 for the answer.

When did East Jersey and West Jersey unite? Page 12 has the answer.

Where was Grover Cleveland born? See page 19 for the answer.

How many inclined planes were along the Morris Canal? Look on page 23 for the answer.

What did Alfred Vail help develop? Page 26 has the answer.

How do flying squirrels fly? Turn to page 28 for the answer.

Where is the Miss America contest held? Look on page 31 and find out!

What state raises more blueberries than New Jersey? Turn to page 32 for the answer.

That was a great trip! We have traveled all over New Jersey!

There are a few places that we didn't have time for, though. Next time, we plan to visit the Camden Children's Garden. This garden features a greenhouse, a carousel, and a maze. There's even a giant sunflower that's 60 feet (18 m) tall!

More Places to Visit in New Jersey

WORDS TO KNOW

colony (KOL-uh-nee) a land with ties to a mother country

culture (KUHL-chur) a people's customs, beliefs, and way of life

ethnic (ETH-nik) relating to a person's race or nationality

gorge (GORJ) land that has been deeply cut by a river

hurricanes (HUR-uh-kaynz) powerful storms that blow in from the sea

industry (IN-duh-stree) a type of business

laboratory (LAB-ruh-tor-ee) a place where scientists work

paperweight (PAY-pur-wate) a heavy object made to hold papers down

reservation (rez-ur-VAY-shuhn) an area set aside for a group of people such as American Indians

New Jersey covers 7,417 square miles (19,211 sq km). It's the 46th-largest state in size.

STATE SYMBOLS

State animal: Horse

State bird: Eastern goldfinch

State dinosaur: *Hadrosaurus*

State fish: Brook trout

State flower: Common meadow violet

State folk dance: Square dance

State fruit: Blueberry

State insect: Honeybee

State memorial tree: Dogwood

State shell: Knobbed whelk (conch)

State tree: Red oak

State flag

State seal

STATE SONG

New Jersey has no official state song. The state legislature voted "I'm from New Jersey" as the state song in 1972, but the governor never signed it into law.

"I'm from New Jersey"

Words and music by Red Mascara

I know of a state that's a perfect playland with white sandy
    beaches by the sea;
With fun-filled mountains, lakes and parks, and folks with
    hospitality;
With historic towns where battles were fought, and presidents have
    made their home;
It's called New Jersey, and I toast and tout it wherever I may roam.
    'Cause . . .

I'm from New Jersey and I'm proud about it, I love the Garden
    State.
I'm from New Jersey and I want to shout it, I think it's simply great.
All of the other states throughout the nation may mean a lot to
    some;
But I wouldn't want another, Jersey is like no other, I'm glad that's
    where I'm from.

If you want glamour, try Atlantic City or Wildwood by the sea;
Then there is Trenton, Princeton, and Fort Monmouth, they all
    made history.
Each little town has got that certain something, from High Point to
    Cape May;
And some place like Mantoloking, Phillipsburg, or Hoboken will
    steal your heart away.

FAMOUS PEOPLE

Abbott, Bud (1899–1974), comedic actor

Aldrin, Edwin "Buzz," Jr. (1930–), astronaut

Basie, William "Count" (1904–1984), piano player, bandleader

Blume, Judy (1938–), children's author

Burr, Aaron (1756–1836), U.S. vice president under Thomas Jefferson

Cleveland, Grover (1837–1908), 22nd and 24th U.S. president

Costello, Lou (1906–1959), comedic actor

Crane, Stephen (1871–1900), author

Edison, Thomas (1847–1931), inventor

Ginsberg, Allen (1926–1997), poet

Harry, Debbie (1945–), singer

Lloyd, John Henry (1884–1965), baseball player

Nicholson, Jack (1937–), actor

O'Neal, Shaquille (1972–), basketball player

Sinatra, Frank (1915–1998), singer

Springsteen, Bruce (1949–), singer, guitarist

Vaughan, Sarah (1924–1990), singer

Whitman, Walt (1819–1892), poet

Willis, Bruce (1955–), actor

Wilson, Woodrow (1856–1924), 28th U.S. president

TO FIND OUT MORE

At the Library

Brallier, Jess M., and Robert Andrew Parker (illustrator). *Who Was Albert Einstein?* New York: Grosset & Dunlap, 2002.

Cameron, Eileen, and Doris Ettlinger (illustrator). *G Is for Garden State: A New Jersey Alphabet.* Chelsea, Mich.: Sleeping Bear Press, 2004.

Klingel, Cynthia Fitterer, and Robert B. Noyed. *Thomas Edison: Inventor.* Chanhassen, Minn.: The Child's World, 2003.

Weatherly, Myra S. *The New Jersey Colony.* Chanhassen, Minn.: The Child's World, 2004.

On the Web

Visit our home page for lots of links about New Jersey:
http://www.childsworld.com/links

Note to Parents, Teachers, and Librarians: We routinely verify our Web links to make sure they are safe, active sites—so encourage your readers to check them out!

Places to Visit or Contact

New Jersey Commerce and Economic Growth Commission, Office of Travel and Tourism
PO Box 820
Trenton, NJ 08625
609/777-0885
For more information about traveling in New Jersey

The New Jersey Historical Society
52 Park Place
Newark, NJ 07102
973/596-8500
For more information about the history of New Jersey

INDEX

*Bye, Garden State.
We had a great time.
We'll come back soon!*